TIME TRAVEL GUIDES

ANCIENT CHINA

Jane Shuter

Chicago, Illinois

© 2007 Raintree
Published by Raintree,
A division of Reed Elsevier Inc.
Chicago, Illinois

Customer Service 888-363-4266

Visit our website at www.heinemannraintree.com

Designed by Steve Mead and Geoff Ward
Photo research by Ruth Blair
Illustrations by Eikon Illustration and Tim Slade
Printed by South China Printing Company

11 10 09 08 07
10 9 8 7 6 5 4 3 2 1

Library of Congress Cataloging-in-Publication Data
Shuter, Jane.
  Ancient China / Jane Shuter.
    p. cm. – (Time travel guides)
  Includes bibliographical references and index.
  ISBN-13: 978-1-4109-2729-3 (library binding - hardcover)
  ISBN-10: 1-4109-2729-6 (library binding - hardcover)
  ISBN-13: 978-1-4109-2736-1 (pbk.)
  ISBN-10: 1-4109-2736-9 (pbk.)
  1. China–Description and travel. I. Title.
  DS707.S56 2007
  931–dc22
                        2006033868

Acknowledgments
The author and publisher are grateful to the following for permission to reproduce copyright material: AKG Images **p. 36** (Erich Lessing); Alamy **pp. 56–57** (imagebroker); Ancient Art & Architecture Collection Ltd. **p. 18** (B. Crisp); Art Archive **pp. 54** (Berry Hill Galleries, NY), **15, 31** (Bibliothèque Nationale, Paris), **24** (Dagli Orti), **27** top and bottom, **40** (Musée Cernuschi, Paris/ Dagli Orti), **17, 28–29, 30** (National Palace Museum, Taiwan), **13**; Bridgeman Art Library **pp. 8** (Arthur M. Sackler Museum, Harvard University Art Museums, USA, bequest of Grenville L. Winthrop), **19** (Bibliotheque Nationale, Paris), **50–51, 44–45** (British Library, London), **48** (Musee Conde, Chantilly, France, Giraudon), **46** (Percival David Foundation, London), **25** (Private Collection), **20–21** (Private Collection, © Christie's Images); Corbis **pp. 43** (Archivo Iconografico), **41, 42, 47** (Asian Art & Archaeology, Inc.), **52** (Bob Krist), **34–35** (Free Agents Ltd.), **10** (John & Lisa Merrill), **38** (Keren Su), **6–7, 11, 37** (Liu Liqun), **47** (Royal Ontario Museum, Canada), **16** (Werner Forman), **53**; Getty Images **pp. 12** (Aurora), **26** (Photodisc), **23** (Stone); Mary Evans Picture Library **p. 55**; Science & Society Picture Library/Science Museum **p. 49**.

Cover photograph of ancient Chinese coins reproduced with permission of Ancient Art & Architecture Collection Ltd./R. Kawka. Cover photograph of Mutianyu on the Great Wall near Beijing reproduced with permission of Corbis/Peter Guttman. Photograph of a bronze figure head reproduced with permission of Corbis/Asian Art & Archaeology, Inc.

The publishers would like to thank Gwen Bennett for her assistance in the preparation of this book.

Every effort has been made to contact copyright holders of any material reproduced in this book. Any omissions will be rectified in subsequent printings if notice is given to the publishers.

CONTENTS

Words that appear in the text in bold, **like this**, are explained in the Glossary.

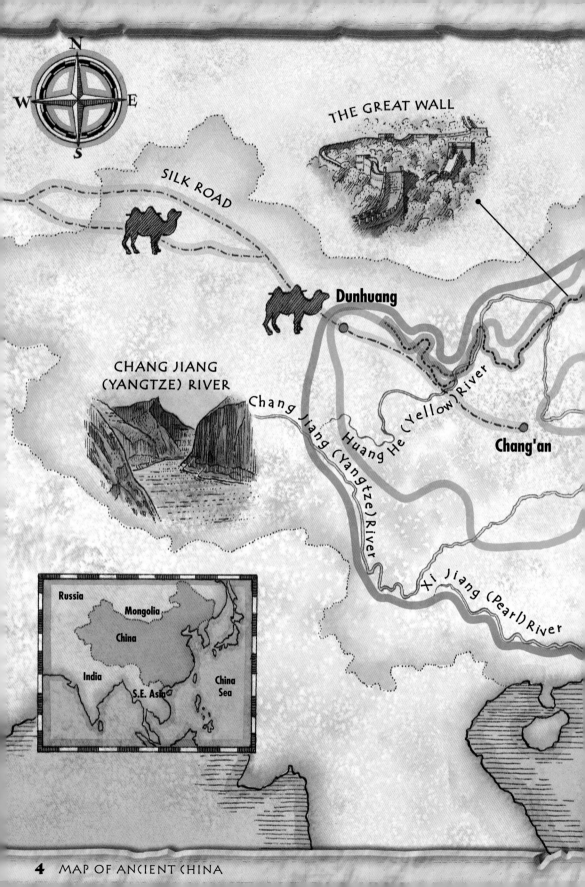

N
W E
S

THE GREAT WALL

SILK ROAD

Dunhuang

CHANG JIANG
(YANGTZE) RIVER

Chang Jiang (Yangtze) River

Huang He (Yellow) River

Chang'an

Xi Jiang (Pearl) River

Russia

Mongolia

China

India

S.E. Asia

China Sea

MAP OF ANCIENT CHINA

Beijing

Tientsin

Hangzhou

THE GRAND CANAL

EAST CHINA SEA

SOUTH CHINA SEA

Ancient Chinese borders

Zia dynasty

Shang dynasty

Qin dynasty

Modern Chinese Border

These amazing sandstone peaks and pillars can be found in south-central China.

CHAPTER 1

FACTS ABOUT ANCIENT CHINA

The period known as ancient China lasts from about 2205 BCE to 1279 CE. That's almost three-and-a-half thousand years! Ancient China is governed by one person, who passes on his power to another family member when he dies. When one family rules for a period, this is called a **dynasty**. The time when the Tang family rules ancient China is called the Tang dynasty, and the period when the Han family rules is called the Han dynasty. The size of ancient China varies depending on how strong these dynasties are. Sometimes the ruling dynasties cannot keep control. These are dangerous times, so choose carefully when you visit ancient China!

WHEN TO GO

The best time to visit ancient China is during the Tang dynasty (618–907 CE), when the ancient Chinese are the most welcoming to visitors. This period is often called the **golden age** of ancient China. You will see lots of great Tang inventions, such as **porcelain**, and find the widest range of goods in the shops. You'll even be able to get a cup of tea!

Another good time to visit is during the Song dynasty (960–1279 CE). Try to arrive around 1000 CE—if you visit any earlier or later, it will be more dangerous. If you're feeling adventurous, you could go right back to the start of the ancient Chinese civilization and visit the Xia dynasty (from about 2205 to about 1818 BCE).

This large **cast** bronze container was made for a Shang tomb. The Shang bronze workers were far more skilled than any other bronze workers in the world at that time.

THE XIA DYNASTY

For a long time, the only evidence of the Xia dynasty was an ancient Chinese history book. Then, in 1959, **archaeologists** found an ancient city, Erlitou, in the area where the ancient book said the Xia ruled. The city was built at the right time, but some archaeologists say Erlitou is really the first city built by the next dynasty, the Shang. Maybe you could discover something to solve the argument!

ANCIENT CHINA – WHEN TO VISIT

(Note: dates given are approximate.)

dynasty	What happened during this time?
Xia (about 2200 – about 1700 BCE)	City of Erlitou built (though this is debated)
Shang (about 1700 – about 1050 BCE)	Magnificent bronzes; silk manufacture begun. China very small at this time, so less variety.
Zhou (1050–475 BCE)	First metal coins are used.
Warring States (475–221 BCE)	Almost constant war between different states.
Qin (221–206 BCE)	First emperor brings peace, but also harsh punishments. Visitors are not welcome and books are burned.
Han (206 BCE–220 CE)	Paper is invented and there is a blossoming of literature. Painted silk **scrolls** are used; ploughs and tools are made from iron.
Three Kingdoms (220–280 CE)	Safe during the early years of this period, but only if you are in the capital of each kingdom.
Period of disunity (265–589 CE)	Almost constant war.
Sui (581–618 CE)	Ancient China united. Grand Canal and other canals built. Lands farthest from the capital are still not safe.
Tang (618–907 CE)	Period characterized by poetry and literature, tea drinking, music, porcelain, and weak emperors.
Five dynasties (907–960 CE)	Almost constant war.
Song (960–1279 CE)	Introduction of paper money, printing, art, exams for **officials**, and the tradition of **footbinding**.

Key:

Stay away — danger!
Okay time to visit
Best time to visit — go for it!

LUNAR FESTIVALS

A good time to visit ancient China is during one of the big festivals. The Chinese calendar is divided into **lunar months** (see page 57). These follow the changes of the moon over 30 days. Check a lunar calendar to find out when the festivals fall in the year you want to travel.

The Chinese New Year (Spring Festival) begins on the first day of the first month of the lunar calendar, usually sometime in late January or early February. It lasts for 15 days and is the longest and most important of the ancient Chinese festivals. When it ends, people light lanterns and watch the moon.

Most festivals are tied to a change in the seasons and have a traditional story associated with them.

- *Qing ming* (the fourth day of the fourth moon) celebrates the start of spring. It is also called tomb-sweeping festival because people clean family tombs on this day.
- *Duanwu* is held on the fifth day of the fifth moon, in mid-summer. Everybody eats rice dumplings steamed in banana leaves. People race boats made to look like dragons, while beating drums. This is to frighten away evil spirits.
- *Zhong Qiu* (the 15th day of the eighth moon) celebrates the harvest. People eat sweet moon-shaped cakes and go out to watch the moon together.

↙ Modern Chinese New Year celebrations also include fast and exciting dragon dances.

BUSY CITY OR PEACEFUL COUNTRYSIDE?

People who prefer a busy city and love to shop should visit the city of Chang'an under the Tang dynasty (see page 39). It is a huge city, well laid out, with two big markets and many smaller ones. The markets are a meeting place for traders from all over China. They sell everything from songbirds to silk shoes.

People who love the peace of the countryside might like to visit the farming villages along the Huang He (the Yellow River). In many places the river is wide and slow. All the land along the river is farmed. Depending on when you visit, you might see farmers guiding ox-drawn ploughs or harvesting their crops. The farmers here grow rice, millet, wheat, beans, vegetables, and **hemp** for cloth. Watch out for the frequent flooding in the rainy season.

If you prefer the sight of steep mountains, take a boat trip along the Chang Jiang (Yangtze) River. Start from the ancient city of Wuhan and go up river.

The mountains along the Chang Jiang River really do rise up this steeply!

GEOGRAPHY AND CLIMATE

Ancient China has a very varied climate and geography, with hot deserts and snowy mountains. The ancient Chinese wear the right clothes for the climate in their area, so dress like the locals. Some places have wide extremes of temperature, especially the deserts. In Dunhuang near the Gobi Desert, the temperature varies from minus 5 °F (minus 50 °C) in winter to over 98 °F (35 °C) in summer.

The variety of climate means there are extreme weather conditions somewhere in ancient China most of the year. Summer **monsoons** in the south bring heat, **humidity**, and flooding. Extreme weather conditions can make travel very difficult. If landslides or floods wipe out roads or bridges, you may be stranded for days or weeks. If you are traveling when there might be extreme weather, take an emergency kit with you. Pack a lightweight tent, a space blanket, dried food, and a bottle of water.

WINTER AND SUMMER WINDS

Everywhere in ancient China is affected by the change of wind direction between winter and summer. Winter winds blow from the north and are cold and dry. Summer winds come from the south and bring warm, wet weather. The rainy season is from May to September. You'll need rainwear everywhere except in the northwestern deserts.

The weather in the mountains can be bitter cold.

FARMING

Most people in ancient China are farmers who live and work on the land of a rich landowner. They mostly live in villages, where they work together in the fields. They have to give some of the crops they grow to the emperor, as a tax. Most of the remaining crops go to the landowner. Any crops they have left after this, they can keep. There is usually just enough to feed the village for a year.

Farmers in ancient China grow a wide variety of crops, depending on the climate and soil where they live. Farmers in the north mainly grow wheat or millet, soybeans, and vegetables such as onions, garlic, and cabbage. In the south, farmers grow crops that need a hot, wet climate, such as rice, red beans, and yam, and tropical fruits, such as kumquats and lychees. Farmers along the Huang He River grow crops, like rice, in the floodwater near the river.

A SPRING CEREMONY

Farming is so important that it has a special spring ceremony. On a day at the start of spring, chosen as lucky for farming, the emperor goes out into the countryside. He makes offerings to the gods and ploughs one **furrow** in a field, to start the planting season.

Modern Chinese farmers grow rice in a very similar way to the ancient Chinese.

GOVERNMENT

Ancient China is ruled by an emperor who has **absolute power**. He makes all the decisions and laws. However, ancient Chinese emperors, especially the later ones, do not think emperors should work. They stay in their palaces and get other people to run the country for them. Early ancient Chinese dynasties use local princes to run different parts of China.

UNDERSTANDING THE SYSTEM

The first emperor, Shi Huangdi, took control of ancient China in 221 BCE. He did not trust the local princes because he thought they might try to take power for themselves. So he divided China into 36 areas. Each area was run by three people: a **military leader**, a **governor** (to run daily life), and an inspector (to make sure the governor and military leader were doing what the emperor wanted). Later emperors use similar systems, with many different kinds of officials. Often several officials are needed to discuss even simple decisions, so decision-making can take a long time.

BE PATIENT!

Try to be patient if you are held up by ancient Chinese decision-making. The ancient Chinese think that losing your temper is extremely rude. Good behavior is so important that laws have been made about it.

ANCIENT CHINESE SOCIETY

Society in ancient China is very strictly organized. The ancient Chinese have very clear ideas about the importance of different people. This depends on how rich people are and, more importantly, what job they do. The most important people are the emperor, nobles, and their families. They are rich and do essential jobs. But farmers are very important, too, despite being poor. This is because they grow the food that everyone needs. Traders are not seen as important, even if they are rich. This is because the ancient Chinese do not feel that trade is important to the country's survival.

This picture shows people taking exams to become officials. You need to be well educated to pass the exams, so you also need a wealthy family to pay for your education.

These women are guests at a feast and concert at the Tang emperor's court. They sit together, not with their husbands.

FAMILY LIFE

To the ancient Chinese, family ties are considered more special than ties of friendship or business. The most important member of a family is the oldest man. Everyone has to obey him, even his adult sons. In return, he is expected to look after the rest of the family, from his eldest son to the least important servant. He has to give them a home, clothes, and food, and he has to educate his children.

SEPARATE LIVES

Although the family is central to ancient Chinese life, families in rich and important **households** actually spend very little time together! They have large homes, with separate living areas for women. The women of the family stay at home, while the men spend much of their work and free time away from the home. Poorer families mix together more. In farming villages, a family lives in one room. But even in these villages, the men spend most of their work and leisure time together, away from the women.

DIFFERENT ROLES

Boys and girls also have a different place in the family. A boy works for his family and takes care of his parents when they are old. He is expected to marry and to have children. Most boys do the same job as their father, and learn by working with him from an early age. Only the sons of wealthy families have an education. They are taught at home by tutors.

Girls are taught to take care of the home and, if their family is rich, to deal with servants. Most girls also learn to make cloth, sew, and entertain. When a girl marries, her parents have to give an expensive gift to the husband's family. Then she goes to live with her husband's family. She does not support her parents in their old age, but takes care of her husband's family instead. All families in ancient China want several sons.

An adult son and his wife and children are greeting his parents. The wife is bringing them breakfast. Children are expected to value and obey their parents all their lives.

BELIEFS

The ancient Chinese believe that a number of gods, goddesses, and spirits affect their everyday life. Nature spirits are thought to have come to Earth either as spirits or as ordinary people. They can bring rain, good luck, or even a toothache!

ANCESTORS

The ancient Chinese have great respect for their **ancestors**. They believe that the spirits of the dead go to an **afterlife** that is just like ordinary life. These spirits are thought to influence life on Earth. So the ancient Chinese look after family tombs carefully, leaving offerings for dead family members. They pray to them, too. They believe their ancestors can help them or, if they are displeased by not being looked after, make life difficult.

This giant statue of the **Buddha** was carved by Buddhist monks living in caves in Yungang. The caves have many statues like this one.

BUDDHISM

During the Han dynasty, a new religion reached China from India, brought by travelers along the Silk Road (see map on page 4). This religion was Buddhism, and it became very popular. The later you visit ancient China, the more likely you are to find that most people are Buddhist. Buddhists practice **meditation**. They believe in treating one another well, and in **reincarnation** after death.

THE SAYINGS OF CONFUCIUS

Most ancient Chinese follow the teaching of the famous **philosopher** Confucius (551–479 BCE). Some of his ideas were even made into laws. Confucianism is not a religion; it is a clear set of rules to follow in daily life. Confucianism says that everyone must behave well to each other, showing *ren* (which means kindness) and care. Ancient Chinese ideas about the importance of family and obeying your elders also come from Confucius. Confucius says that if everyone follows his rules, society works well. Emperors must rule wisely, and their people must obey them. In the same way, a father should take care of his household and the household should obey him.

DAOISM

At the same time as Confucius, Lao Tzu taught the ideas of Dao, or "the way." Daoism says that people should live in harmony with each other and with nature. Daoism has become a religion. It includes praying and meditating at special **shrines** in beautiful places.

This picture shows Lao Tzu riding on a water buffalo. The ancient Chinese think it is lucky to meditate while looking at a statue of Lao Tzu.

This group of scholars is enjoying an outdoor meal in a bamboo garden.

CHAPTER 2

PRACTICAL INFORMATION

The ancient Chinese do not travel much, unless they are traders or officials. Most people are born, live, and die in the same place, or within a few miles of it. The ancient Chinese see travel as dangerous, difficult, and unnecessary. Even so, you can travel by road and river, and there are places to stay in villages and towns. The later you travel during the ancient Chinese period, the more choice you will have of places to stay.

WHAT TO WEAR

Because of the varied climate in ancient China, what you wear will depend on where you visit. It is probably best to take lots of light layers with you or, even better, to buy silk clothes when you arrive. Silk is thin and light. It can keep you warm or cool, depending on the weather.

ANCIENT CHINESE CLOTHES

Everyone in ancient China wears a similar style of clothes—several layers of robes wrapped around the body and tied at the waist. Clothes vary according to social class.

- Wealthy women and men wear long robes and silk shoes. These make it diffcult to walk. If you want to go out, you will need to hire a **litter** to carry you. If you are staying in the countryside, you will need to hire a horse.
- Workers wear short robes with trousers underneath.
- Poor people wear clothes made of hemp, not silk. The hemp cloth is usually woven at home.

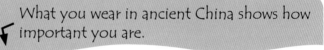
What you wear in ancient China shows how important you are.

Nobleman and his wife   Worker   Poor man

WOMEN'S FASHIONS

The richer a woman's family, the more complicated her clothes, hairstyle, and hair **ornaments** are. It takes a lady in a noble family several hours to dress and put her makeup on each morning!

FOOTBINDING

In ancient China, tiny feet on women are seen as beautiful. During the Tang dynasty (618–907 CE), people start to **bind** the feet of girls to make them even smaller. When girls are about five years old, their feet are wrapped very tightly in bandages. This footbinding turns the toes over, back toward the heel. The toes bend and often break. The bandages are only taken off to put clean ones on. Footbinding makes feet tiny, but they hurt and are difficult to walk on. Because women with bound feet cannot walk far or work, bound feet are a sign of belonging to a wealthy family.

MONEY

The early ancient Chinese do not use money—they **barter**. The first money is cowrie shells, used from the Shang dynasty (1500–1050 BCE) onward. Metal coins are initially used during the Zhou dynasty (1050–475 BCE). The earliest coins are in the shape of spades, knives, and other useful things that are often used to barter with. At first, different parts of ancient China have completely different money. It is not until the time of the first emperor (221–210 BCE) that everyone in ancient China uses the same coins.

These circular coins come from a range of ancient Chinese dynasties.

COINS WITH HOLES

If you travel to ancient China before the time of the first emperor, your money will be heavy and hard to carry. In a later period, you will use circular coins with a hole in the middle. The hole makes the coins lighter, and you can carry them by threading them onto a string. This can then be tied around your waist or to your belt. Be careful in towns, though. Thieves may cut the string and run away with your money.

SWAP SHOP

It's always worth trying to barter, especially in the countryside and small towns. Many poorer people still prefer the ease of swapping a chicken for a bowl, or a cabbage for some rice.

PAPER MONEY

The ancient Chinese are the first people to use paper money. They call it flying money because it is light and can blow away. The first paper money is used during the Tang dynasty (618–907 CE). It is just for travelers and traders, to stop them from being robbed on their journey. It is a piece of paper from one bank that can be exchanged for money at another bank. This swap can only be done by the person whose name is on the paper.

Paper money that can be used by everyone (and does not have names on it) is first used during the Song dynasty (960–1279 CE). However, you will need to remember to check the date printed on the note, because it cannot be used after this date. It is also easily copied, so there is a lot of fake money around.

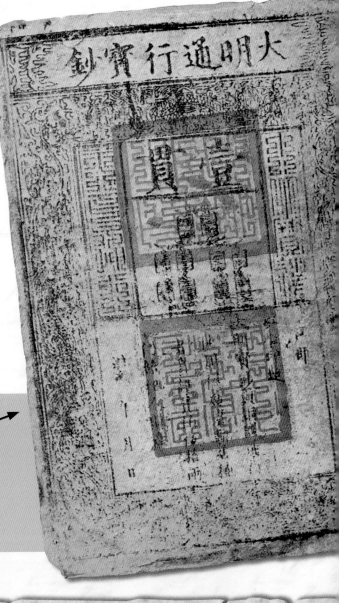

This piece of flying money is one of the oldest surviving examples. It is from the 13th century, a little bit later than the period we call ancient China.

FOOD

Wherever you go in ancient China, the food is amazing! In the north, where wheat is the main crop, people eat a lot of noodles and dumplings. In the south, people eat mainly rice-based dishes.

MEALS FOR RICH AND POOR

Rich people in ancient China eat a huge amount of meat. Vegetables are seen as food for people who cannot afford meat. On special occasions, the rich eat unusual meats, such as snakes and carefully prepared small birds. Everyday meats include pork, chicken, lamb, goose, and duck.

Poor people eat either rice or porridge made of wheat and vegetables. They do not eat meat very often. The poor in the countryside eat better than the poor in towns, because they can grow some food of their own. They also eat meat when, for example, one of their chickens stops laying eggs and they kill it.

CHOPSTICKS ARE FUN!

If you want to eat in ancient China, you need to know how to use chopsticks. (You may know already!) Hold them as shown in the photograph. Then keep the bottom chopstick steady, while moving the top one to pick up the food. "Anything that walks, crawls, or flies with its back to heaven is edible." [An ancient Chinese saying.]

EATING OUT

The ancient Chinese eat their main meal in the evening. Breakfast is often leftovers from the night before, eaten cold. If you are in town during the day, you can snack on food from street **vendors**. They sell everything from plain noodles to rich stews. You can eat the food from the vendor's bowls while sitting on mats in the street.

Simple pottery bowls like this one are used by ordinary people and some street vendors.

At dinner, the meal is placed in the middle of the table and people help themselves. Everything is shared. The ancient Chinese eat quickly at everyday mealtimes. But they will spend a long time over special meals to celebrate a festival or a wedding.

Tea was used as a gift to the gods in religious ceremonies. It was not drunk widely until the Tang dynasty (618–907 CE).

MIND YOUR MANNERS!

It's fine to hold your bowl close to your mouth to eat, but the ancient Chinese think that only people with bad manners scoop the food in with chopsticks. You must never, ever, leave your chopsticks in your food points-first, with the ends sticking in the air. This is how rice is presented as a gift to the dead at funerals, so it is very bad manners in everyday life!

This ancient Chinese picture shows several types of transportation. Oxcarts, horses, and litters are good ways of getting around.

CHAPTER 3

GETTING AROUND

For your journey to ancient China, you will need to know how to get around and where to stay. Because ancient China covers such a huge area, it takes a long time to get from one place to another. The journey will also be uncomfortable. The ancient Chinese do not travel much, unless they are traders. They see travel as difficult and dangerous, and believe that spirits and demons add to the hardships along the way. So don't be surprised if you are warned about robbers and demons when you ask for directions!

TRAVELING BY ROAD

Ancient Chinese roads are earth tracks; there are no paved streets. The first emperor (221–210 BCE) had a few roads made across ancient China, so his officials and army could move around. These are the best roads. They are wider than other roads, and the earth is packed down hard. This means they turn to mud less quickly in wet weather. Many roads in the countryside are very narrow. In the mountains they can be extremely steep.

If you travel by road you can walk or ride a horse. Wealthy people travel short distances in a litter carried by servants. If you are walking, you might be lucky and get a lift in an ox cart. Ox carts are very slow, but this is how many farmers and some traders move their goods. Camels are the usual means of transport along the Silk Road (see map on page 4), and people travel in large groups wherever possible. This cuts down on the chances of getting lost or being attacked by robbers.

LIGHTING THE WAY

You can only travel by day in ancient China. There is no street lighting, and the roads are hard to follow at night even with a full moon. Mountain roads are not only steep and narrow, but also wind around. This can almost double the distance you have to travel.

TRAVELING BY BOAT

Wherever possible, the ancient Chinese travel by water. They use rivers, canals, and if traveling along the east coast, the sea. From the Sui dynasty (581–618 CE) on, you can travel on the Grand Canal, which joins the Huang He and Chang Jiang rivers. It is over 1,000 miles (1,600 kilometers) long, 10–30 feet (3–9 meters) deep, and 100 feet (30 meters) wide in places. Work started on the canal in 70 CE. It is repaired all the time, and is still in use today.

For short river or canal journeys, you can use local ferryboats. They run on a timetable from ferry stops. The most important ferries have a ferry guard on the landing to take your money. He can tell you how long the journey will take and where to get off. For longer journeys or sea journeys, you will need to talk to the captains of boats at the **quayside**. Many trading ships will take passengers, although you may be expected to sleep on deck or in the **hold** with the goods.

The second Sui dynasty emperor, Yangdi, is shown traveling on the Grand Canal.

WHERE TO STAY

When traveling in ancient China, you can stay at several different kinds of inns. In the cheapest inn you will have to share a room with other travelers. The inn may be just one large room where everyone eats and sleeps, with a separate kitchen building. There are not likely to be washing facilities, toilets, or bedding.

In more expensive inns there will be separate rooms for eating and sleeping. In the most expensive inns you may get a room to yourself. You will probably be given water for washing, and there will be toilets a short walk from the main building. Most inns also provide some kind of food and drink.

AN HONORED GUEST

If you are lucky, you might be invited to stay at an ancient Chinese family's home. This is considered a great honor because family homes are very private. The comfort you enjoy will depend on the wealth of your host family, but as a guest you will always be given the best of everything they have.

CHOOSING A GIFT

If you stay in a family home, you should take a gift. But be careful! A cheap gift is considered rude, and an expensive gift is seen as showing off. The best kind of gift is something over which you have taken time and effort, such as a poem. If you stay in a village, you should buy enough food for the whole village to enjoy. This could be anything from a sack of rice to a whole pig, depending on your budget.

↖ This is a typical home of a noble family.

Noble families live in big homes built around two (or more) courtyards. The first courtyard and the rooms around it are for entertaining visitors. The rear courtyard is for the women and children of the family. Noble families have plenty of servants. If you stay for a few days, the servants will wash your clothes for you, taking them to the nearest river and beating them with rocks.

LIFE IN A VILLAGE

In a village, families live in a one-room house. They will either have a fenced-off section of the room for their animals, or the animals will live in a shed at the side of the house. Most village life goes on outdoors, in the fields, or in the main square of the village. In a small village, almost everyone will come from the same family.

The modern Great Wall follows the line of the ancient Great Wall.

CHAPTER 4

THINGS TO DO IN ANCIENT CHINA

Wherever you go in ancient China, there's lots to see and do, from a restful break in the countryside to tours of the cities and shopping expeditions. You'll find something to suit all tastes and budgets. There are also some "must see" places for an unforgettable trip. And whatever you do, don't forget to visit the Great Wall.

THE GREAT WALL

The Great Wall is an amazing achievement. It forms a huge barrier between ancient China and the outside world. If you drew a straight line from one end of the Great Wall to the other, it would cover 1,678 miles (2,700 kilometers). However, the Great Wall makes big loops and, in some places, there are up to three extra pieces of wall, one behind the other. The workers who built the Great Wall actually built 4,160 miles (6,700 kilometers) of wall.

The Great Wall was not built all at once. Early Chinese rulers built pieces of wall to keep out invaders from the north. The first emperor (221–210 BCE) was the ruler who decided to build a wall right along the northern boundary.

The original Great Wall was built of earth, rammed down hard in layers with pebbles, reeds, or wood. Over the centuries, the earth is replaced with stone. In the 21st century, the Great Wall is made entirely of stone.

GREAT WALL FACTS

Length: 4,160 miles (6,700 kilometers)

Workers: criminals — thieves, murderers, people who owned books banned by the first emperor

Deaths among workers: about 1 death for every 5 feet (1.5 meters) of wall

Additional workers: elephants did some of the heavy lifting

The countryside around the Great Wall has huge contrasts, from snowy mountains to flat farmland.

PEACE AND QUIET

Why not combine your trip to the Great Wall with a few days of rest and relaxation in the nearby countryside? You could experience the cold, calm northern mountains or the magic of a night in the desert, completely dark except for your campfire and the stars.

If you like to be quiet and meditate, you are in luck. The ancient Chinese believe in meditating in especially beautiful places. You will be able to find small inns in beautiful places all over the ancient Chinese countryside. The owner may be able to recommend particularly beautiful spots nearby.

Or perhaps you would prefer to travel along one of ancient China's many rivers? The fishing is good, and river travel can be peaceful and soothing. It can be exciting, too! One ancient Chinese poet described a river journey in a storm this way: "The water rises in a huge mass and falls, foaming and frothing."

THE PEACE OF THE COUNTRYSIDE

"Floating on the river are shining insects,
The reeds and grasses on the banks
    reflect in the water.
My heart feels peaceful and calm
The slow clear stream is pleasing."
        [From an ancient Chinese poem.]

DUNHUANG

These are temples in the caves near Dunhuang.

Dunhuang is a city on the Silk Road at the western edge of ancient China. It's a very old walled city, full of traders and visitors from many different countries. The streets of Dunhuang are always busy, and you will hear many different languages spoken here. Traders often travel in large groups, so they are less likely to be robbed. Groups of traders often block the streets with anything from 10 to 100 heavily loaded camels. Some visitors stay at Dunhuang to become more familiar with the ancient Chinese language and **culture** before moving farther into China.

Dunhuang is also famous as a meeting place for Buddhist monks and **scholars**. From the Han dynasty (206 BCE–220 CE) on, many Buddhist monks and scholars settled in the caves in the mountains at Dunhuang. Here, there are many shrines and temples to Buddha.

THE POSTAL SERVICE

Dunhuang is part of an ancient Chinese postal service that serves many cities. Official government messengers take letters across all parts of ancient China, both to and from the emperor. However, this service only runs inside ancient China. If you want to send letters home, you will have to pay traders at Dunhuang who are traveling in the right direction.

CHANG'AN

Chang'an is very different from Dunhuang. The cities are at either end of the Silk Road inside ancient China (see map on page 4), but Dunhuang is a trading city, while Chang'an is a city of emperors. Trade is allowed only in one part of Chang'an. The emperor and his officials are much more important. During the Han dynasty (206 BCE–220 CE), more than half the city is just palaces for the emperor!

During the Tang dynasty (618–907 CE), Chang'an is a huge city, with a population of more than a million. Chang'an is carefully planned on a grid pattern, so it's hard to get lost. It is also organized into different areas, with palaces and official buildings walled off from the rest of the city. Because the city is well planned, you probably won't stray into the wrong areas, but be especially careful to avoid the imperial area. You could be executed if caught!

WHAT TO SEE IN CHANG'AN

This is a plan of the city of Chang'an. The markets are the biggest attraction for visitors. Look out for the high **watchtowers** at the gates and on the corners. Take a walk around the city walls, but don't try to walk all the way. It's a trip of over 20 miles (32 kilometers)!

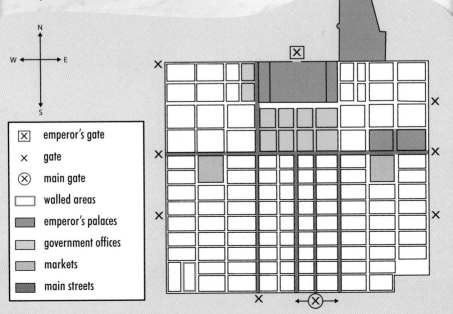

N
W ← → E
S

⊠   emperor's gate
×   gate
⊗   main gate
▢   walled areas
▨   emperor's palaces
▨   government offices
▨   markets
▨   main streets

ENTERTAINMENT

Most entertainment in ancient China happens in the street. Go to the marketplace and you'll find musicians, singers, acrobats, jugglers, and dancers. The shows are free, but be prepared to give something, as this is how the street performers make their living. You are more likely to find entertainment in towns. The bigger the town, the better the street entertainment is likely to be.

Street entertainers like the audience to join in. So sing along with the singer, or gasp if an acrobat does something spectacular. You can move from performance to performance, and no one expects you to be quiet. On the contrary, most of the audience will be chatting.

CAGED BIRDS

The ancient Chinese love to keep caged birds. In many towns, the owners of caged birds meet regularly in certain teahouses. Being together really does seem to make the birds sing more. So you will be able to sit and drink tea while watching and listening to the birds.

Acrobats were a popular decoration on bowls and cups. Wealthy people often had pottery models of acrobats buried with them.

WATCH OUT FOR PICKPOCKETS

Take care of your belongings! You are in the most danger of being robbed while watching street performers. It is easy for robbers to escape through the crowds and the small alleys of the towns.

PRIVATE SHOWS

For most wealthy people in ancient China, entertainment is a private thing. Emperors and nobles have their own musicians, dancers, and acrobats. If you are lucky enough to stay with a noble family, you will probably see a performance after dinner. Less wealthy people hire street musicians, dancers, and acrobats for special occasions.

Another form of entertainment is writing poetry and then reading it aloud to family or friends. Many wealthy people also enjoy making music. Girls from wealthy families are taught to play several musical instruments, sing, and dance. They at least have to learn to play the *samisen*, a sort of guitar.

MUSICAL INSTRUMENTS

Ancient Chinese musicians play a huge variety of musical instruments. They group their instruments by the material they are made from:

- *silk*: any instrument with strings (the strings are made from silk)
- *bamboo*: flutes and pipes
- *wood and stone*: instruments that are hit
- *clay*: drums and a kind of mouth organ
- *gourd* (fruit or vegetable hollowed out and dried): mouth organ
- *hide*: drums.

These are some of the 65 bells found in the tomb of a governor from the Zhou dynasty (1050–475 BCE). The bells weighed almost 3 tons (3,050 kilograms) and were perfectly tuned. Each bell could make two notes, depending on where you hit it.

GAMES

Almost everyone in ancient China enjoys playing games. Dominoes, backgammon, go, and mah jong are all being played by the end of the period. The ancient Chinese also invented card games, including poker. Playing cards is a very popular pastime for wealthy ladies. It can also be used to break the ice when meeting new people.

BETTING

The ancient Chinese like to gamble. They bet on the outcome of sporting events and all kinds of games, even between friends.

Try playing ancient Chinese dominoes! In its simplest form, it is very similar to the modern game. However, the ancient Chinese often play with two sets of dominoes at a time, one with pictures and one with numbers. The rules for playing with two sets are complicated and people play very fast. You may leave very confused!

The ancient Chinese often carry games in their large sleeves, so they can play with them if they are kept waiting for any reason.

Many ancient Chinese also enjoy word games, such as finishing quotations or making up poetry on the spot. These games give wealthy people a chance to show off their education. Poor people don't play games like this, and they don't have much leisure time. However, they do enjoy dominoes.

Nobles enjoy playing **polo**, which came to China from India.

SPORTS

The ancient Chinese enjoy sports. People in villages or in the poorer areas of towns are most likely to go to **cock fighting** matches. Nobles like to hunt wild animals on their estates. They also practice archery and **fencing**. These have been popular sports for centuries because they provide valuable skills during times of war.

ANCIENT CHINESE INVENTIONS?

Many people claim the ancient Chinese invented these sports:

- Soccer, known as *t'su chu*. Chinese soccer has two teams. It uses a leather ball stuffed with silk, and then filled with air. There are rules about not using your hands, and (sometimes but not always) a net for scoring goals.
- Golf, known as *chiuwan*, is very popular in the Song dynasty (960–1279 CE). Chinese golf has tees, holes in the ground marked with a flag and a stick (similar to a modern green), and golf clubs with bamboo handles and hard wooden heads.
- Badminton, which is played by two people who hit a bird (a feathered shuttlecock) to each other, trying to keep it in the air.

In ancient China, shops line the main roads in and out of towns. Most shops are the front part of the shopkeepers' homes, with workshops behind them.

CHAPTER 5

SHOPPING

Ancient Chinese towns and cities are full of shops and markets. Markets are usually the best place to buy the goods that China is famous for, such as silk, porcelain, and **jade**. You can pick up a real bargain from a silk trader. There are also many things using ancient Chinese technology that you can buy very cheaply. These will amaze your friends when you return home!

TRADITIONAL SOUVENIRS

SILK

Silk is used in ancient China to make clothes, bedding, and rope. It can also be written and painted on. The market silk stores have many different colors for you to choose from. But you won't find any yellow silk for sale. Only the emperor and his family can wear yellow.

The ancient Chinese make a lot of money from selling silk to other countries. This is because, up until just before the Sui dynasty, only they know how to make it! When ancient China is threatened, the emperor can often stop an attack by giving silk as a present. How to make silk is a carefully guarded secret. If a silk merchant reveals the secret, he could be imprisoned or executed.

PORCELAIN

Another great souvenir to buy in ancient China is porcelain. Porcelain is a type of pottery that is especially hard and smooth, and often very thin. Like silk, only the ancient Chinese know how to make porcelain, so they can trade it at a high price. People outside ancient China prefer thin, white porcelain. Inside ancient China, the most expensive porcelain has a **glaze** that is cracked on purpose. If you want to buy some porcelain, the best time to visit is during the Song dynasty (960–1279 CE).

The cracks in this Kuan ware dish are made on purpose to make it look interesting.

LACQUER

Another famous ancient Chinese product is **lacquer**, which is used to make many different things, such as combs, trays, and bowls. Lacquer is made from the **sap** of the lacquer tree. It is very useful because it cannot be damaged by heat or water.

It takes a lot of skill and time to make even a simple lacquer bowl. First, the sap is colored with ground-up rock. Then it is painted onto objects made of wood or stone. It has to be put on in layers, and each layer has to dry completely, which takes about two days. Some of the most beautiful and expensive pieces of lacquer could have as many as 200 coats.

A GOOD PRESENT
A small lacquer bowl makes an excellent present. Lacquer is beautiful and very shiny. It is also light and less fragile than porcelain.

JADE

Jade is a precious stone that the ancient Chinese use to make jewelry and ornaments. It is very hard, so is difficult to carve and shape. Even a simple bracelet with no patterns can take several days of hard work to make.

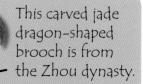

This carved jade dragon-shaped brooch is from the Zhou dynasty.

AMAZING GIFTS

There are lots of gifts you can buy to show your friends how amazing ancient Chinese technology is. The ancient Chinese are very inventive, and you can pick up small, light, and interesting gifts quite cheaply. Many of the inventions suggested below are from the Tang or Song dynasties.

PAPER

If you are traveling from the Song dynasty (960–1279 CE) on, why not take some paper home? Paper was invented in Han times (206 BCE–220 CE) but was not widely used until much later. If you want to copy some ancient Chinese writing or painting, you'll need to buy brushes and ink as well. Ink is sold as a heavy, solid brick. You'll need to grind some ink off the block and mix it to the right thickness with water. Other paper items, such as a beautiful lantern or kite (see box), also would make good gifts. Or you could take home a pack of ancient Chinese cards or a mah jong set and teach your friends to play!

FLY YOUR KITE

The ancient Chinese make beautiful, detailed kites. Even the cheapest one looks elegant when it flies. Some kites are shaped like dragons and butterflies. These have complicated string systems, to make the kite move like a dragon or butterfly as it flies.

WATER CLOCKS AND FIRECRACKERS

A beautiful, fascinating, and very unusual present is a water clock. Water flows from a tank into 36 buckets on the wheel at a regular rate. As the buckets move around filling and emptying as they turn, they move the clock mechanism. They mark off different periods of time depending on how long the wheel takes to turn.

To make your return home go with a bang, you could take some fireworks. The ancient Chinese invented gunpowder in Tang times. At first, it was used in war, but by the Song dynasty it was used to make fireworks. You can even buy fireworks on tiny skis that shoot along the ground or across water. These are called ground rats and water rats.

The magnetic compass spread all over the world from ancient China, where it was first used during the warring states (475–221 BCE). The ancient Chinese called it a south pointer.

WHEEL IT HOME

Ancient China offers many shopping opportunities, so it's possible that you will buy too much to carry home! If you're traveling from the Han dynasty (206 BCE–220 CD) on, you can take your presents home in a wheelbarrow—another ancient Chinese invention.

This Chinese doctor is taking his patient's pulse to check her health.

CHAPTER 6

HEALTH AND SAFETY

While visiting ancient China, you will need to stay healthy and safe on your travels. The most usual emergencies while traveling are needing a doctor or being the victim of a crime. Lucky for you, medicine in ancient China is very advanced, and the crime rate is low. Be careful not to commit a crime, though. The crime rate is low for a reason— punishments are very harsh!

> Chinese medicine in the 21st century still uses herbal treatments similar to those used by the ancient Chinese.

STAYING HEALTHY

To stay healthy in ancient China, you must drink only clean water. Rivers and streams in the countryside are fine to drink from, especially if they are fast moving, but water from rivers in towns is less safe. This is because people throw garbage into the river and sometimes use it as a toilet. You can often cure an upset stomach by eating nothing but plain boiled rice or noodles for a day or two.

If you need a doctor, it is best to go to the biggest nearby town, where there will be several doctors to choose from. The easiest way to find a doctor is by asking someone—the ancient Chinese visit their doctors several times a year. Doctors usually work at home, although they will come to your inn or the house you are staying in. If you get sick in the countryside and can't get to a town, you will have to rely on the villagers. Most villages have one person who knows about herbal cures.

HOW TO PAY

Many ancient Chinese pay their doctors to keep them well. They visit them regularly and take any medicines prescribed. If a person gets stick, the doctor is not paid because the doctor has failed to keep the person healthy.

ANCIENT CHINESE MEDICINE

Ancient Chinese medicine is based on the flow of energy, or *qi* (say "chee"), around the body. If you are well, the ancient Chinese say that your energy flows smoothly. If you are unwell, the energy is said to be blocked in some way. Ancient Chinese doctors believe that what you eat, how you exercise, and how you think affects your *qi*. The aim of all ancient Chinese medicine is to get your *qi* flowing well. Doctors check *qi* by feeling the pulse in your arm. They treat it with herbal medicines and acupuncture.

HERBAL CURES

Ancient Chinese herbal cures are still in use in the 21st century. For example, the ancient Chinese used willow bark for pain relief. Modern aspirin is a chemical version of willow bark.

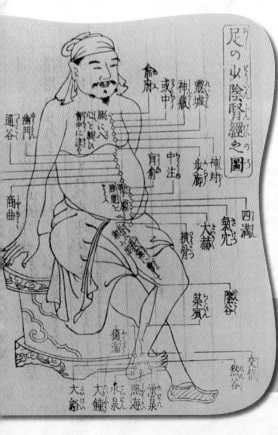

ACUPUNCTURE

Acupuncture is done by inserting needles into the body at certain points to get the *qi* flowing again. It can look scary, but don't worry —it isn't painful. You might feel a tingle similar to the feeling of pins and needles, or you may feel something like a sharp tug. But if your doctor is well trained, you should not feel any pain.

This diagram shows just a few of the 360 acupuncture points that an ancient Chinese doctor has to learn.

STAYING SAFE

To stay safe in ancient China, you should use good sense. When watching a street performance or shopping, keep your money in a safe place. Don't hang your money string on your belt. Behave politely and remember that giving way to people who are better dressed than you (and so of a higher class) is actually a law.

The ancient Chinese legal system is clearly structured. You will need to report any crime to the local **magistrate**. He has police, officials, and doctors to help him investigate. If the criminal is caught, the person is found guilty only if he or she confesses to the crime. The magistrate and his helpers are allowed to beat, or even torture, a criminal to get a confession.

POLITE LAWS

From the start of the Qin dynasty (221 BCE), laws are not just about stopping crime, such as theft. They

This magistrate is investigating a person accused of a crime. The magistrate sits at the table. The other people near the platform are his officers, and the man with a stick is a policeman.

EXECUTIONERS
Executioners are usually soldiers. They take pride in beheading a criminal as quickly as possible. They wear yellow silk aprons to show that they are acting for the emperor (usually only the emperor can wear yellow).

are also about making people follow rules for polite behavior. For instance, respect for your elders is enforceable by law. A girl who is shown to have insulted her parents can be strangled to death.

A RANGE OF PUNISHMENTS

Punishments range from a beating (the least severe punishment) to beheading (the most shameful execution). Minor criminals are often made to wear a wide wooden collar called a *cangue*. The person wearing it can still move around and work with difficulty, but must depend on others to feed him or her. Pickpockets are beaten, then **branded** on the arm for the first two offenses. After that, they have to spend three years doing hard work. Armed robbers are executed.

This photo, taken in the 1890s, shows a cangue. Women were often put in the cangue for not being respectful enough to their mothers-in-law or husbands.

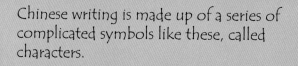

Chinese writing is made up of a series of complicated symbols like these, called characters.

CHAPTER 7

ANCIENT CHINA FACTS AND FIGURES

This section will provide you with a handy reference guide for your trip to ancient China. You can look up the various dynasties and some important inventions. You can also check out the dates of the major festivals, and some books and websites that will help you find out more about ancient China.

ANCIENT CHINA PHRASE BOOK

WRITTEN ANCIENT CHINESE

Since the time of the first emperor (221–210 BCE), ancient China has had one written language. This language does not translate into an alphabet—it is a pictograph system. This means that characters are merged with each other to make a new word. So, for instance, if you put the characters for *mouth* and *man* together, you get the character for *elder brother*. Chinese characters change depending on the time you want to visit. (See the examples below.)

SPOKEN ANCIENT CHINESE

Although ancient China has only one written language, there are many spoken languages. Most of these rely as much on the tone of what you say as the word you are saying. So a word can have several meanings, depending on whether you start high and drop your voice, start low and raise your voice, keep the tone level, or move the tone around. Some people find this musical treatment of language easy to pick up, but others have trouble hearing the difference.

	Shang	Zhou	Warring States	Qin onwards
rén (nin) human				
nu(nra?) woman				
er (nha?) ear				
ma (mra?) horse				
yú (nha) fish				
shan (sran) mountain				
rì (nit) sun				
yuè (not) moon				
yu (wha?) rain				
yun (wan) cloud				

WRITTEN NUMBERS

The way numbers are written in ancient China also changes over time. Here are examples from the Shang dynasty (1500–1050 BCE).

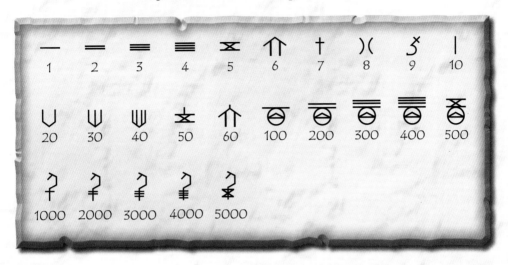

Toward the end of the Han dynasty (206 BCE–220 CE), officials start to use counting boards. These boards are rows of nine squares. Little rods of bamboo or ivory are put in the boards to show numbers. From this point, people begin to write numbers in a way that reflects their use on a counting board (see below).

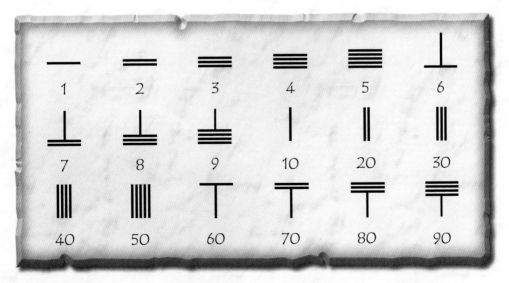

ANCIENT CHINA AT A GLANCE

TIMELINE

Xia (2205–1818 BCE)	City of Erlitou is thought to be built.
Shang (1500–1050 BCE)	Bronze working is very advanced. The first writing is created.
Zhou (1050–475 BCE)	Confucius is teaching.
Warring States (475–221 BCE)	The Zhou Kingdom is broken up into a number of different kingdoms. They fight each other. The Kingdom of Qin grows in power.
Qin dynasty (221–207 BCE)	First emperor introduces the same currency, weights, measures, and writing across China. Great Wall is built on the northern border.
Han dynasty (206 BCE–220 CE)	Buddhism reaches China. Paper is invented.
Three Kingdoms (220–280 CE)	China is broken into three kingdoms. First book printed.
Period of disunity (265–589 CE)	The three kingdoms break up into more kingdoms.
Sui dynasty (581–618 CE)	Buddhism grows in popularity. Grand Canal is built. Porcelain is invented.
Tang dynasty (618–907 CE)	Tea drunk widely for the first time. Gunpowder invented.
Period of disunity (907–960 CE)	Gunpowder used in war.
Song dynasty (960–1279 CE)	Introduction of paper money, printing, art, exams for officials, and the tradition of footbinding.
1279 CE	Mongols from the north take over ancient China. They settle and create their own dynasty, the Yuan.

THE LUNAR CALENDAR

The lunar calendar follows the changes of the moon. The months have no names and are called first moon, second moon, and so on.

- 12 months = 1 year
- 30 days = 1 month
- 1 week = 10 days

DATES OF FESTIVALS

The Chinese New Year (Spring Festival) begins on the first day of the first month.

Qing Ming begins on the fourth day of the fourth moon.

Duanwu begins on the fifth day of the fifth moon.

Chong Yang begins on the seventh day of the seventh moon.

Zhong Qiu 15th day of the eighth moon.

Dong Zhi at the winter solstice (day of least sunshine) in the 11th month.

Laba the eighth day of the 12th moon.

FURTHER READING

BOOKS

DuTemple, Lesley. *The Great Wall of China*. Minneapolis: Lerner Publishing Group, 2002

Landau, Elaine. *Exploring Ancient China With Elaine Landau*. Berkeley Heights, NJ: Enslow Publishers, Inc., 2005

Hodge, Susie. *Ancient Egyptian Art*. Chicago: Heinemann Library, 2006

WEBSITES

- http://www.historyforkids.org/learn/china/
- http://mnsu.edu/emuseum/prehistory/china/

GLOSSARY

absolute power people with absolute power make all the decisions and have to be obeyed

afterlife where you go when you die

ancestor someone from your family who lived before you

archaeologist person who excavates (digs up) historical sites very carefully and studies what he or she finds

barter to exchange things of a similar value, rather than use money

bind wrap up very tightly

branded mark burned on something or someone with a hot iron

Buddha Indian spiritual teacher who lived in the 6th century BCE. His name means "the enlightened one."

cast make hard metal into a new shape by melting it

cock fighting male chickens (cocks) fighting each other

culture way of life typical of people living in a particular time and place

dynasty period of time when a single family rules a country

fencing fighting with swords

footbinding tying up girls' feet tightly to make them smaller

furrow narrow trench made in the ground by a plough

glaze glass-like surface on pottery

golden age period of time when a country is at its wealthiest, is well governed, and is making new discoveries in many things

governor person who runs part of a country for the ruler of the country

hemp plant that has stems that can be used to make rope or cloth

hold (of a ship) place at the bottom of a ship where things are stored

household everyone living in the same house; the family and their servants

humidity dampness in the air

jade hard, bluish-green precious stone

imperial to do with an emperor, king, or royal empire

lacquer shiny coating made from the sap of the lacquer tree

litter large seat with curtain all around that is carried by poles underneath

lunar month month that follows the 28-day movement of the moon

magistrate someone who decides if a person has broken the law, and can decide punishment for the person if guilty

meditation calming the mind by focusing attention on something simple, such as breathing or an image

military leader person in charge of an army

monsoon season of heavy rains

official person working for the government

ornament object used for decoration

philosopher someone who studies the purpose of life

polo sport in which a ball is hit into a goal by people riding horses. The people on horseback hit the ball with a long stick.

porcelain type of pottery made with kaolin, which can be baked at a high temperature until very hard and smooth

quayside place where ships tie up to the land

reincarnation coming back to life on Earth as a different person, animal, or thing

sap juice inside a plant or tree

scholar someone who studies a particular subject

scroll long, thin roll of paper or fabric

shrine special place to worship

vendor someone who sells something

watchtower high, protected place where soldiers can keep watch

INDEX